MATERIALS
AND THEIR PROPERTIES

SERIES EDITOR
REBECCA HUNTER

www.heinemann.co.uk/library

Visit our website to find out more information about **Heinemann Library** books.

To order:
☎ Phone 44 (0) 1865 888066
🖹 Send a fax to 44 (0) 1865 314091
💻 Visit the Heinemann Bookshop at www.heinemann.co.uk/library to browse our catalogue and order online.

First published in Great Britain by Heinemann Library, Halley Court, Jordan Hill, Oxford OX2 8EJ, part of Harcourt Education. Heinemann is a registered trademark of Harcourt Education Ltd.

Produced for Heinemann Library by Discovery Books Ltd
Editorial: Nick Hunter and Jennifer Tubbs
Design: Ian Winton
Production: Viv Hichens
Picture research: Maria Joannou

Originated by Ambassador Litho Ltd
Printed in Hong Kong, China by Wing King Tong

ISBN 0 431 17441 5 (hardback)
06 05 04 03 02
10 9 8 7 6 5 4 3 2 1

ISBN 0 431 17445 8 (paperback)
07 06 05 04 03
10 9 8 7 6 5 4 3 2 1

British Library Cataloguing in Publication Data
Hunter, Rebecca
    Materials and their Properties. - (Explore Science)
    530
A full catalogue record for this book is available from the British Library.

Acknowledgements
The publishers would like to thank the following for permission to reproduce photographs: Andrew Lambert: page **43**; Corbis: pages **9**, **15**; Getty Images: page **30**; Jeff Edwards: page **21**; Oxford Scientific Films: pages **6**, **8**, **10**, **12**, **32**, **39**; Photodisc: pages **14** (top), **36**, **41**; Robert Harding Picture Library: **17**; Science Photo Library: pages **4**, **5**, **7**, **11**, **13**, **14** (bottom), **16**, **20**, **22**, **25**, **26**, **27**, **28**, **31**, **33**, **34**, **35**, **38**, **40**, **44**; Trevor Clifford: pages **18**, **19**, **23**, **24**, **29**, **37**, **42**, **43**.

Cover photograph of a volcano reproduced with permission of Science Photo Library.

The publishers would like to thank Angela Royston for her contributions to the text of this book.

Every effort has been made to contact copyright holders of any material reproduced in this book. Any omissions will be rectified in subsequent printings if notice is given to the publishers.

Any words appearing in the text in **bold**, like this, are explained in the glossary.

Contents

Groups and classifying materials

What are materials?

Materials are the different kinds of ingredients that things are made of. Wood, stone, **plastic** and **metal** are examples of materials. Every object in the world is made of a material. For example, the things you play with are probably made of plastic or metal. Your home is probably made of stone or bricks, with wooden doors and glass windows.

Some things are made of just one material. A table may be made only of wood. Many toys are made only of plastic. But most objects are made of several different materials. A bicycle has a metal frame and rubber tyres. A computer has a plastic case, but some of the parts inside are made of **silicon**, or metal.

You can see many different materials in this classroom. They include wooden table tops, metal table legs, paper books and plastic trays.

Using materials

People have always used the materials they find around them to make other things. Rocks from the ground are used to build homes. Trees are cut down to make furniture, doors and floors. Parts of plants and animals can be used to make clothes.

The materials that this bicycle is made of were carefully chosen. The metal frame is strong but light. The rubber tyres are bendy and squashy when they are filled with air. A bicycle with metal tyres and a rubber frame would not work.

When designers and engineers are planning how to make something, they have to decide what materials they are going to use. Each material has different **properties**. Some are strong, some are bendy, some are hard and others are soft. Some **melt** easily and some are waterproof.

Natural and synthetic materials

Natural materials come from things that are found in the natural world around us. They include materials from plants, materials that come from animals and materials that are found in the ground. Many natural materials have to be changed in some way before they can be used. Metals have to be separated from the rocks they are found in. Glass is made by heating sand. **Synthetic materials** are made by scientists from **oil** and other **chemicals**.

 ## Exploring further

You can find out more about how we make and use different materials on the Heinemann Explore CD-ROM. Follow this path: Contents > Digging Deeper > Materials technology

Materials from plants

Wood

Wood comes from trees and is a **natural** material. Different kinds of trees produce different kinds of wood. Broad-leaved, **deciduous** trees, such as walnut and oak, give **hardwoods**. These woods were used in the past to build houses. Hardwoods also look attractive and are used to make good quality furniture but they are expensive and take a long time to grow.

Softwood comes from **coniferous** trees such as pines and firs. Most new wood comes from softwood trees that have been specially grown. These trees grow quickly with tall, straight trunks. When they are cut down, they are taken to a sawmill to be cut into long, flat planks. Softwoods are much lighter and cheaper than hardwoods and have many uses.

Properties and uses of wood

- Wood is light and strong and is easy to cut and shape. This makes it useful for furniture, floors, window frames and many other things around the home. Wood also has the unusual quality of being able to be carved. Furniture, such as tables and chairs, often has carved wooden legs.
- Wood is fairly flexible, or bendy. This makes it a good material for floors. It is comfortable to walk on. Dance floors and theatre stages are made out of wood – its springiness gives dancers more lift.

Softwood tree trunks are taken to a sawmill and are stored ready to be cut up into planks of wood.

Many things around the home are made of wood. The outsides of these houses are made almost completely from wood.

- Unprotected wood rots easily, particularly if it is damp. Wood that is in the open air, such as window frames or outside doors, needs to be protected by a layer of paint or **varnish**. Insects such as termites and woodworms can also attack wood, but they can be killed with **chemicals**.

- Wood floats in water and for many centuries has been used to build boats. About 150 years ago, iron ships started to replace wooden ones. Today rowing boats, yachts and other small boats may still be made of wood, although a **synthetic material** called fibreglass is often used instead.

- Wood burns easily, but it does not **conduct** heat. It is a **thermal insulator** and can be used to protect people or things from heat. Pan handles are sometimes made of wood. While the pan gets hot, the handle is still cool enough to hold.

- Wood is not a **conductor** of electricity either.

Exploring further – Paper

Paper is also made from wood. Follow this path on the CD-ROM to find out about how we make and use paper: Exploring > Grouping and Classifying Materials > Paper

Cotton

Cotton is the most commonly used **natural fibre**. It comes from cotton plants. Cotton cloth is used for bed sheets, curtains, clothes, tablecloths, towels and many other purposes.

The white fluffy balls on a cotton plant are made by the cotton seeds and show that the plant is ready to be harvested.

 How is cotton made?

Cotton plants produce a 'boll' of seeds each with a fluffy fibre. Cotton wool is made from cotton fibres. It is soft and easy to pull apart. Cotton thread, however, is strong. It is made by combing and straightening the fibres and then twisting them to make one long, strong thread. This process is called spinning. Cotton thread is then woven to form cloth.

Properties and uses of cotton

- Cotton is woven into different kinds of cloths or **fabric**. Denim is one of the strongest types of fabric. It is used to make jeans, which are very hard-wearing. Jeans were first made as working clothes for gold miners and labourers. They later became fashionable for young people.

- Cotton easily takes in water and so is a good material for towels and cloths. Cotton clothes **absorb** sweat, the film of moisture that covers your skin. This makes cotton clothes more comfortable to wear than **synthetic materials** such as **nylon**. They are cool in summer and warm in winter.

- Dyes are used to make cotton cloth in many different colours. The cotton absorbs the dye and takes on its colour. Some dyes are made from plants such as indigo (a blue dye), others are made from **chemicals**.

- Cotton washes and dries well. It can be washed in a washing machine and boiled to get it really clean. Clothes that have been dyed may need to be washed more carefully. Sometimes the dye in the cloth leaks out (or 'runs') when the cloth is washed.

- Cotton cloth which has been washed usually looks creased. It has to be ironed to smooth out the creases.

Each of these rolls of cotton cloth have been dyed different colours and printed with various colourful patterns.

Exploring further – Digging deeper

You will be surprised at just how many natural sources of materials there are. The CD-ROM contains charts that shows where other natural materials come from and their many uses. Follow this path: Contents > Key Ideas > Grouping and Classifying Materials

Other materials from plants

Rubber

Rubber is made from the **sap** of the rubber tree. A slit is made in the bark of the tree and the sap oozes out. It is collected in special cups.

Rubber is also waterproof and **airtight**. This means that water and air cannot pass through it. Surgeons, dentists and nurses wear latex rubber gloves to keep their hands clean of blood, water and germs in the air. Rubber is hard-wearing as well as waterproof. This makes it a good material for boots and raincoats.

Sap oozes from the bark of a rubber tree. The sap is collected in cups and sent to the factory to be made into latex sheets, which are then made into rubber products.

? Why is rubber used for car tyres?

The main special quality of rubber is its flexibility. This makes it very useful for tyres for cars, lorries, buses and bicycles. The tyre is filled with air. When the vehicle goes over a bump in the road, the tyre squashes and then bounces back into shape. No other material does the job so well.

One of the main uses of cork is to seal liquids in bottles. The cork fits so snugly into the bottle, that it has to be prised out with a corkscrew.

Cork

Cork comes from the bark of the cork oak tree. The cork is stripped from the trunk of the tree without killing the tree. Some of cork's many useful properties are listed here.

- It is a very light material because it has many trapped pockets of air. It easily floats on water and is made into floats for fishing nets and into floating buoys. It also used to be used in life-jackets and life-belts.

- Cork can be easily squashed but bounces back into shape again. It is hard-wearing and the Romans used to put it on the soles of their sandals. It would have been a comfortable, springy material to walk on.

- Cork does not easily take in water and so is used as a stopper for bottles of wine. The cork is squashed as it is pushed into the top of the bottle. As it tries to bounce back into shape, it makes an airtight and watertight seal.

- Cork is a bad **conductor** of heat and so can be used as an **insulator**. Table-mats are often lined with cork to protect the table from hot plates and dishes.

Exploring further – Rope

Rope is another material made from plant fibres. Find out more about it on the CD-ROM. Follow this path: Exploring > Grouping and classifying materials > Other material from plants

Materials from animals

Wool, silk and leather are the most common materials that we get from animals.

Wool

Most wool comes from sheep. After the long fleece is sheared off the sheep, it is then sorted, cleaned and combed into straight strands. The strands are then twisted and spun into woollen yarn. Woollen yarn is either knitted into jerseys and other clothes, or it is woven to make a woollen **fabric**.

Sheep farmers usually shear their sheep once a year, but in some places the sheep are sheared twice.

Properties of wool

- Wool is soft and flexible and easy to sew or knit with.
- It is a good **thermal insulator**, and wearing woollen clothing is the best way to keep warm.
- Woollen cloth, such as tweed, is hard-wearing and is made into suits, jackets and skirts.
- Wool can be washed and does not crease easily.

Silk

Silk is made by silkworms. Silkworms are bred on special silk farms. The silk moth lays eggs that hatch into caterpillars. Each caterpillar forms a cocoon by producing a fine silk thread that it winds round and round its body. The cocoons are collected and the silken threads unwound. Several threads are twisted together to give a stronger thread.

When the silkworm is fully grown, it spins a cocoon made of fine silken thread.

Properties of silk

- Silk thread is very strong. It is stronger than a strand of steel of the same thickness.
- Silk is also stretchy so it is very good for making into clothes.
- Silk clothes are very light to wear. Before **synthetic materials** were invented, silk was the lightest, finest fabric.
- Silk is cool in summer, but in winter it is warmer than cotton, **rayon** or other light fabrics.

Exploring further – More materials from animals

Discover more about another useful material that we get from animals – leather. Follow this path: Exploring > Grouping and classifying materials > Materials from animals

Stone and glass

Stone comes from rocks in the ground. It is dug out of the ground in quarries. Solid stone can be used to build houses, walls and bridges. Crushed stone, or gravel, is used with other materials to make tarred roads and concrete.

Special machines cut huge slabs of solid rock from quarries.

Stone is strong, heavy and hard-wearing. It does not rot or burn, and it **melt**s only at extremely high **temperatures**. It is not a good **conductor** of heat.

There are many different kinds of stone. Granite, marble, slate, limestone and sandstone are those most commonly used in building. They each have different special properties which makes them useful for a variety of things.

Concrete

Concrete is the most common building material today. It is made by mixing cement (a **mixture** of lime and clay) with water and sand or gravel. When it is wet, it can be moulded into any shape. It hardens as it dries into a very tough stone-like material. It is cheap to make and is used in buildings, bridges, dams and almost all large structures.

? **What are precious stones?**

Precious stones are rare and beautiful crystals found in some rocks. The crystals have to be carefully cut to give them a clear colour and perfect shape. Precious stones are used in jewellery, but some are also used in industry. This precious stone is a ruby. Rubies are red and are very hard-wearing.

The front of this building is almost completely made of glass. The glass is supported by strong steel frames.

Glass

Glass is a unique material. It is made mainly from sand which is mixed with soda and lime and heated to a very high temperature (1200° to 1600° Celsius). At this temperature, the mixture melts and becomes a clear, thick but runny liquid. When the liquid cools it forms hard, clear glass. Coloured glass is made by adding a coloured **chemical** to the mixture.

Glass has to be shaped while it is still very hot and partly melted. It can be made into sheets of glass for windows or poured into moulds to make lenses. Glass-blowing is a special art and a way of making hollow or special shapes from glass.

Properties of glass

- Glass is transparent, which means you can see through it. This makes it ideal for windows.
- It is waterproof. It would be no use in windows if it did not keep rain-water out!
- Glass is cheap and easy to make and it can also be recycled.
- It is strong and **hygienic** and is often used as a container for food and drinks.

Exploring further – Pottery and bricks

Pottery and bricks are both made of clay which is dug from the ground in quarries. Find out more about the manufacture and uses of pottery and bricks on the CD-ROM. Follow this path: Exploring > Grouping and classifying materials > Pottery and Bricks

Iron and steel

Iron and steel are two of the most commonly used **metals**. Iron is a **natural** material that's found in rocks as an ore. An ore is a metal which has combined with another substance. Iron is made by heating iron ore with coke (a form of carbon from coal), and limestone. When this is done, much of the carbon can be removed to make steel.

Henry Bessemer (1813–98)

Henry Bessemer invented a way of producing steel from iron cheaply. Steel is a purer form of iron, made by burning off much of the carbon contained in iron ore. Bessemer realized that steel could be made quite simply from molten iron by blowing very hot air through it. The hot air burned off the carbon and other impurities. This process became known as the Bessemer process and made Henry Bessemer one of the richest and most celebrated engineers of his day.

Uses of iron and steel

Iron has been used for 4000 years to make knives, swords and other tools and weapons. Nowadays, iron and steel are used to build bridges, blocks of flats and offices, cars, trains and railway tracks. They are also used to make many smaller everyday things, such as knives and forks, cans, paper-clips and safety-pins.

Iron has to be heated to 1535° Celsius before it **melts**. People working with the iron have to wear special clothing to protect them from the high **temperatures**.

Thick steel cables take the weight of this suspension bridge over the River Severn.

Properties of iron and steel

- Both iron and steel are very hard and strong. Steel and iron beams are used to build the frames of many modern buildings. Steel is also made into thick cables that are strong enough to hold up a suspension bridge.

- They are both waterproof, which means they have many diverse uses ranging from ship building to making kitchen sinks.

- Iron and steel both **rust** easily. They can be protected from rust by painting them or by coating them with a layer of zinc (galvanizing) or chromium (electroplating). Stainless steel does not rust.

- Both iron and steel can be made into **magnets**. Anything that is made of iron or steel will be attracted to a magnet.

- Iron and steel can be made into many different shapes from heavy iron beams to thin wire.

- Many iron and steel products can be recycled. Drinks cans in particular are often recycled. They are separated from cans made of a metal called aluminium by using a magnet.

 Exploring further – Precious metals

Find out about other metals and the three precious metals, gold, silver and platinum, on the CD-ROM. Follow this path: Exploring > Grouping and classifying materials > Other metals

Synthetic materials

Plastics

Plastics are **synthetic materials** made from **oil**. An amazing material, plastic can be made into many different things. It is cheap to produce and can be made to look like glass, leather, metals, wool, cotton and many other more expensive materials.

How plastic is made

Today almost all plastic is made from oil. Oil is a thick liquid that is found naturally in the ground. It is processed and separated into different substances. Petrol is one substance that we get from oil; plastic is another.

All of these things have been made from plastic. Plastic can be brightly coloured to make it look fun and attractive, or it can be clear and see-through.

Properties of plastic

- Plastic can be poured into moulds to make many different shapes such as plates, cups, toys, bottles, buckets or furniture.

- Plastic can be made into a rigid shape that does not change, such as a computer, or it can be flexible and bendy as in polythene sheets.

- Plastic does not conduct electricity at all. This makes it a good **insulator**. Electrical wires are covered with plastic to make them safe.

- Plastic can also insulate against heat, although it can **melt.**

- Plastic is **airtight** and watertight – it does not let water or air pass through it. Plastic wrappers are used around food to keep out air and damp.

- Plastics float in water.

- Plastic does not **rust** or rot, which is both an advantage and a problem. Slides, swings and seesaws are made of plastic so that they will last a long time. But plastic is very difficult to get rid of when it is no longer needed.

- Most plastic things that are thrown away do not decay. However, some plastics can be recycled and some new plastics are **biodegradable**.

Synthetic fabrics

Synthetic fabrics are manufactured from **chemicals**. They include **nylon**, polyester, acetate and **rayon**. They are widely used in clothes, bedding, curtain material, carpets and sofa coverings.

Rayon is made from cotton while acetate is made from cellulose, a material made from plants. Rayon feels much like cotton but is easier to wash and iron. Acetate feels more like silk. Nylon, polyester and acrylic are made from chemicals, mainly from oil. Most synthetic fibres burn easily. Those that are used for children's clothing and for furniture should be treated with other chemicals to make them flame resistant.

95% acrylic
4% nylon
1% Lycra® elastane

AE121223
56011

RESHAPE WHILST DAMP

Every garment is labelled to show the materials it includes. Many clothes are made of a mixture of synthetic materials and cotton.

Exploring further – Fabrics

Find out more about the qualities and uses of synthetic fabrics on the CD-ROM. Follow this path: Exploring > Grouping and classifying materials > Synthetic fabrics

Changing materials

Solids, liquids and gases

Matter is everything that exists in the world. Matter includes rocks, water, plants, animals and air. All matter is either a **solid**, a **liquid** or a **gas**. These are called the three **states** of matter. Each state has different properties.

Everything in the world is either a solid, a liquid or a gas. Here the ice is solid, the water is liquid and the water vapour is gas. The air around it all is also a gas. You cannot see air, but you know it is there.

Solids

Solids keep their shape. You can feel their shape with your fingers and, when you pick them up, their basic shape does not change. A piece of cotton thread might change from an S-shape to a straight line, but the actual thread itself does not change shape. Solids can be cut or broken into more than one piece.

Liquids

Liquids do not have their own shape. Instead they take the shape of the container they are in. Liquids are runny and can be poured from one container to another. A liquid flows from one place to another and it always flows downhill. You cannot cut or break a liquid. Water is the most important liquid for all living things.

Gases and vapours

Gases and **vapours** are nearly the same thing and most are invisible. Gases and vapours do not have their own shape. They mix with air and spread out into all the space they can. For example, a bottle of perfume contains liquid perfume, but the space above it is full of perfume vapour. When you take the top off the bottle, the perfume vapour moves out of the bottle into the air and into your nose. When you smell the perfume, you are smelling the vapour.

Molecules

All matter is made of tiny particles called **molecules**. Molecules are made up of **atoms**, the very smallest particles of an element that can exist. Each kind of material has its own combination of molecules. Molecules are so small you cannot see them, even under the strongest microscopes. Just a small amount of material consists of billions of molecules.

A substance is a solid, a liquid or a gas, depending on how close together its molecules are and how fast they are moving. In a solid, the molecules are packed so close together they hardly move at all. In a liquid, the molecules are a bit further apart and slowly swirl around each other. In a gas, the molecules are moving so fast they do not stay together at all. They spread out into any empty space. The diagram below gives you an idea how molecules in different states behave.

This diagram compares molecules in a solid, liquid and gas. In a solid, the molecules are tightly packed. They are bound together and hardly move at all. In a liquid, there is more space between the molecules and they are free to move around within the liquid. In a gas, the molecules move very fast and are not attached to each other at all.

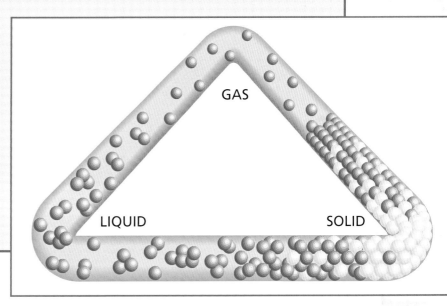

Exploring further – Animation of molecules

See what happens to the molecules in a gas as a material cools down in the animated film on the CD-ROM. Follow this path: Contents > Key Ideas > Grouping and classifying materials

Air and other gases

Air is a **mixture** of **gases**. The Earth is surrounded by a layer of air. You cannot see air, but you can feel it. Wind is moving air. You can feel it blowing against your face when you run hard. You can see what wind does: it can blow the branches and leaves off trees and it pushes the clouds through the air.

Trapped air

Air is lighter than **liquids** and all the **solid** things that make up the Earth. If you fill a solid with air, it becomes lighter than it would be if it were solid all the way through. Balls are filled with air to make them light and bouncy.

When you blow up a balloon, you are blowing air into it. The balloon stretches as more air is blown in.

A bathroom sponge has many holes in it. The holes are filled with air. When you put the sponge in water, it floats. When you push the sponge into the water and squeeze it, you can see the bubbles of air leave the sponge and rise to the top of the water. The spaces in the sponge are then filled with water. The sponge becomes heavier.

You cannot see air, but when it moves you can feel it and see the effect it has. Here, a particularly strong gust of wind has blown this woman's umbrella inside out!

Living things need air

Life on Earth would not be possible without air. Air contains **oxygen**, a gas which all living things need to breathe in order to survive.

This girl is inflating a balloon by blowing air into it.

The main gases in the air are nitrogen, **oxygen**, **carbon dioxide** and water **vapour**. Nearly three quarters of air is made up of nitrogen. About one quarter is oxygen. Animals breathe in oxygen and breathe out carbon dioxide.

Plants use carbon dioxide to grow and give out oxygen. Burning uses up oxygen. When wood, coal or **oil** burns, the carbon in these materials is changed to the gas carbon dioxide.

(?) How does air protect us from the heat of the Sun?

Air does not conduct heat very well. This means that when the Sun shines, only some of its heat reaches us. Without air, the ground would be too hot for most things to survive during the day. Air also keeps heat in. It is like a blanket around the Earth. Without it, the Earth would be freezing cold at night.

Exploring further – Other gases

Discover more about other gases and their uses on the CD-ROM. Follow this path: Exploring > Grouping and classifying materials > Air and other gases

Mixing solids and liquids

Materials can be mixed with other materials in several different ways. **Solids** can be mixed with solids. **Liquids** can be mixed with other liquids. And solids can be mixed with liquids.

Mixing solids

Solids can be mixed together when each is in many separate small pieces. Grains of rice, for example, can easily be mixed with peas. Sometimes the best way to mix solids is to grind them into powders first.

Mixing liquids

Most liquids mix together fairly easily. Watery liquids will mix well with each other, but not with oils or fats, which are lighter than water. If you pour some cooking oil into water, mix it with a fork and then leave it, the oil will float back to the top.

Mixing solids and liquids

Only some solids mix well with water. If you add sand to a container of water, the sand will sink to the bottom of the container. If you add soil to a container of water, the soil will make the water turn cloudy but most of it will sink to the bottom, leaving only tiny particles of clay **suspended** in the water.

This is one method of grinding a solid to a powder. You can also do this with herbs and spices.

Making a solution

If you add salt to water and stir it, it disappears or **dissolves**. The salt has mixed so well with the water it has become part of the liquid. The new liquid is called a **solution**. Salt dissolves in water to make a salt solution. Many things dissolve in water. Sugar dissolves in hot tea (which is mainly water).

The more salt there is in a solution, the stronger or more 'concentrated' it becomes. Water can only hold a certain amount of salt before the solution becomes **saturated**. If you then try to add more salt to the water, it will not dissolve.

A few drops of ink quickly spread through water.

How do you make solutions weaker?

If you add water to a solution it **dilutes** it. This means that it makes it weaker or less concentrated. Fruit squash or cordial is a concentrated solution of fruit drink. You have to dilute it by adding water.

Exploring further – Why materials change

All the materials that we use are acted upon and changed by many outside forces. Discover how and why things change on the CD-ROM. Follow this path: Contents > Digging Deeper > Changing Materials

Reversible changes

Heating up

When you heat a **solid**, such as chocolate, it **melts**. It changes **state** from a solid into a **liquid**. Changes of state are **physical changes**. They do not involve the **chemical** make-up of the material. The chocolate looks and feels different, but it is still the same substance.

Heating causes two physical changes. Heat makes a solid change into a liquid. This is called melting. And heat makes a liquid change into a **gas**. This is called **evaporation**. Physical changes are **reversible**. When the melted chocolate cools down, it changes back into a solid.

As the candle burns, the wax around the wick warms up and begins to melt. Eventually, some of the hot liquid wax will spill over the edge of the candle and trickle down the side. It cools down and becomes a solid once more.

Melting

The **melting point** is the temperature at which the material melts and becomes a liquid. Every kind of material has its own melting point. Ice-cream soon melts when it is taken out of the freezer. Its melting point is lower than room **temperature**. Butter and chocolate are solid at normal room temperature, but they do not have to be heated very much before they begin to melt. Most metals have to be heated in especially hot furnaces before they melt. Temperatures deep inside the Earth are so high that even rocks become **molten** and runny. They pour out when a volcano erupts.

Evaporating

When a liquid is heated, the particles begin to move faster. Some have so much energy they escape from the surface of the liquid and **evaporate** into the air becoming a gas. Some liquid products need to evaporate in order to achieve their purpose. If you spread a layer of nail **varnish** over your nail, the liquid soon evaporates and the varnish becomes hard and dry.

Boiling

The more a liquid is heated, the faster it evaporates. Eventually the liquid begins to **boil** and the liquid begins to change to gas. Bubbles of gas form in the liquid and rise to the top and burst. This is the **boiling point**. Each liquid has its own boiling point. The boiling point of water is 100° Celsius. The liquid will never get hotter than its boiling point. But the more you heat it, the faster it changes to a gas.

The water in this pan has reached its boiling point. The bubbles are bubbles of water **vapour**.

Exploring further – Changing temperatures

Learn more about the effects of changes in temperature on different materials. Follow this path on the CD-ROM: Contents > Digging Deeper > Changing Materials > Temperature changes

Cooling down

When a **liquid** becomes cold enough it changes **state** and becomes a **solid**. Water **freezes** and changes to solid ice. Like **melting**, this is a **physical change**. It does not involve the **chemical** make-up of the material. Although ice looks and feels different, it is made of the same substance as water.

Cooling causes two physical changes. When gases are cooled, they change into liquids. This change is called **condensation**. And when liquids are cooled, they change into solids. When melted candle wax trickles down a candle, it cools and changes back into solid wax. This is called **solidifying** or freezing.

The water in this pond has become so cold that some of it has frozen into ice.

Gabriel Daniel Fahrenheit (1686–1736)

Gabriel Fahrenheit was the first person to make a **thermometer** using mercury. At first he used many different scales for recording temperatures, but eventually he adopted a scale based on the freezing point and boiling point of water. The scale is called Fahrenheit, after him. Today we use the Celsius scale of temperature, invented by a Swedish scientist called Anders Celsius. See Exploring further.

Freezing

The **temperature** at which a material changes from a liquid to a solid is called its **freezing point**. Some liquids have a higher freezing point than others. Water freezes to ice when it reaches O° Celsius. However, alcohol needs to be much colder than this before it freezes. Most metals freeze at a very high temperature, which is why they are solids at normal room temperature. The **melting point** and the freezing point of a material are the same. Ice starts to melt at O° Celsius and water starts to freeze at O° Celsius.

Condensing

When water **vapour condenses** it changes back to water. The air is a **mixture** of gases, including water vapour. When air becomes colder, some of the water vapour changes back into water. When a kettle boils, lots of steam escapes into the air. The things above or near the kettle become covered with drops of water. The water is steam that has condensed when it hit these cooler surfaces.

When you blow on to a cold mirror, the glass becomes covered with a thin film of water droplets. The water has condensed from water vapour in your breath.

Exploring further – Celsius

Find out about Anders Celsius and the temperature scale that is named after him on the CD-ROM. Follow this path: Contents > Biographies

The water cycle

A cycle is something that goes round and round. On Earth the water cycle keeps the land supplied with fresh water. Water from the sea and the land makes rain. The rain falls onto the land and drains into rivers and back into the sea to begin the cycle again. The cycle works because water changes from **liquid** to **gas** or **vapour** (**evaporation**) and then from vapour back to liquid water (**condensation**). These two **physical changes** – evaporation and condensation – keep the water cycle going.

Clouds gather over the hills near a lake. When the water droplets in the clouds become heavy enough a rain shower occurs.

Making rain

As the sun warms the Earth, the water on the surface changes into water vapour and drifts up into the air. Water evaporates from the surface of rivers, lakes and puddles, but most water evaporates from the surface of the seas and oceans. As the water vapour rises, it cools. As it cools, it condenses to form clouds of tiny water droplets.

The wind blows the clouds across the sea and over the land, and they collect more and more water droplets. They become heavier and many of the droplets join together to make bigger drops. When the cloud meets colder air or has taken in too much water, these drops become too heavy to float in the air and fall to Earth as rain.

Rainforests have their own water cycle. Trees release water vapour through their leaves. It rises into the air, making it misty and damp. Much of the water vapour forms huge thunderclouds. Every day rainstorms soak the forest, providing a fresh supply of water for the trees.

? Where does drinking water come from?

The water you drink comes from lakes, reservoirs (artificial lakes), springs and wells. The water that runs out of your taps may have fallen as rain only a week ago or it may have fallen years ago. Bottled water usually comes from springs in the ground. These are places where water that has been trickling through the rocks, perhaps for thousands of years, comes to the surface. Many people think that spring water tastes better than tap water, but scientists say that it is often no different. Whichever water you drink, it has been recycled through the water cycle for millions of years.

Exploring further – Water and its uses

Water is the most common substance on Earth. Discover how important it is to us on the CD-ROM. Follow this path: Digging Deeper > Solids, Liquids and Gases > Water

Irreversible changes

Physical changes are **reversible** changes. When a liquid is cooled, it **solidifies**, but if the **solid** warms up, it changes back into a liquid. Similarly when a **gas** is cooled, it **condenses**, but if the liquid is then heated, it changes back into a gas.

A **chemical reaction** cannot be reversed. The material is changed into a different substance and cannot be changed back. Cooking, **rusting** and burning are all examples of **chemical changes**. When you boil a raw egg, the white becomes hard, and the yellow yolk becomes thicker. You cannot take a cooked egg and change it back to a raw egg. When a piece of wood burns, you cannot change the ash back to wood. It is an **irreversible** change.

Some reactions happen slowly, others happen more quickly. Rusting is a slow reaction while cooking is faster. Burning is a very fast reaction.

Rusting

Rusting is a slow chemical change. Iron and steel rust. The **metal** slowly reacts with **oxygen** and water in damp air to form a new substance called iron oxide, which is what we call rust. The damper the air, the quicker the metal rusts.

The surface of this iron ship is covered with rust. The rust is a different substance from the iron. It cannot be changed back into clean iron again.

Cooking

When you cook food such as meat, fish and vegetables, it slowly changes. Cooking makes meat and fish taste better and easier to eat. It also kills off most of the germs and makes them safe to eat. Meat and fish look different when they are cooked. Red meat becomes browner and fish changes from semi-translucent to white or pink. Vegetables can be eaten raw or cooked. Cooking makes them softer and easier to chew, but it destroys some of the vitamins in them.

When eggs, bacon and tomato cook they each go through chemical changes. You can see the changes, but you cannot reverse them. The egg white, for example, changes colour and becomes a solid.

Not all cooking involves a chemical change. When you **melt** butter or chocolate, you are producing a physical change, not a chemical change. When the butter or chocolate cools down it will change back to a solid. Cooking sometimes involves melting butter or fat which is then used in a chemical change. When you make a cake, you mix the flour, sugar, butter and eggs together. The **mixture** could be separated into its ingredients again, although it would be difficult. It is only when you cook it that a chemical change takes place. The soft, runny mixture becomes a soft, spongy solid. There is no way of changing a cooked cake back into the uncooked mixture.

Exploring further – Compounds and mixtures

You can find out more about how atoms behave in compounds and mixtures on the CD-ROM. Follow this path: Contents > Digging Deeper > Separating Materials > Compounds and Mixtures

Burning

Burning is a fast **irreversible** change. It is one of the fastest **chemical reactions**. Burning occurs when heat makes a substance combine with **oxygen** from the air to give at least one new substance. Wood is mainly carbon. When it burns, the carbon combines with oxygen to make **carbon dioxide**. When a substance burns it produces heat. There are several reasons why we burn things – to get heat, light, energy or power, or to get rid of rubbish. We burn **fuel** to light and heat our homes, to cook with, to make electricity and to move cars, trucks and other forms of transport.

As this match burns a chemical reaction is taking place. For this reaction to happen there must be oxygen in the air. When you blow out a match you cover the flame with carbon dioxide from your breath. This leaves no room for the oxygen so the match goes out.

Fuel for light and warmth

In the past, people burned mainly candles and oil lamps to give them light at night. Today we use electricity to make light bulbs glow brightly. But many power stations burn fuel to make the electricity.

Antoine Laurent Lavoisier (1743–94)

Antoine Lavoisier is said to be the founder of modern chemistry. He discovered that when something burns it combines very fast with a gas in the air. He carefully weighed the substances before and after they burned and found that they had gained weight. He concluded that the extra weight was caused by the substances combining with air.

People have burned wood and coal for thousands of years to get heat. Coal is the concentrated remains of forests that grew millions of years ago. It produces more heat than wood, but it also produces a lot of smoke and **chemicals** that pollute the air. Today most homes burn **natural gas** or **oil** to heat their water and run their central heating.

This incinerator is used to burn rubbish. It reduces the rubbish to a convenient pile of ash, but at the same time it releases carbon dioxide into the air.

Making electricity

One way of making electricity is to heat water to make steam. (The steam drives a machine that generates electricity.) Coal, oil or natural gas are burned to heat the water. Although burning oil and natural gas do not produce as many **pollutants** as burning coal, they still produce huge quantities of carbon dioxide. This is the main gas that causes **global warming**.

Fuel for transport

Almost all vehicles burn petrol or diesel oil in their engines. When petrol and oil burn, they produce carbon dioxide, water **vapour** and other gases, many of which pollute the air. Engineers are trying to find other fuels that will not damage the **atmosphere**.

Exploring further – Biographies

Learn more about Antoine Lavoisier and his experiments in chemistry. Follow this path on the CD-ROM: Contents > Biographies

Separating mixtures of materials

Separating solids

Solids may be mixed with other materials in different ways. Solids may be mixed with other solids, **liquids** or **gases**. Soil, for example, is a **mixture** of materials in all three **states**. Pond water is a mixture of different substances, including decayed plants, fine sand and mud and water. A cup of tea may be a mixture of water, tea, milk and sugar.

Gold is sometimes discovered among gravel at the bottom of streams and valleys. For many years, people have panned for gold. They roll the gravel in water around the pan and pick out any pieces of gold.

Separating a mixture of solids

Sometimes we need to separate one or more of the materials from the rest of a mixture. If the pieces of solid are large, they may be sorted by hand. If you have a box of different coloured beads or different buttons, the easiest way to sort them is by hand. But if you had a mixture of salt and uncooked rice, it would take hours to separate them by hand.

Some solids can be separated using a sieve. A sieve is a wire mesh. Cooks usually shake flour through a sieve to get rid of the lumps. A sieve can also be used to separate a powder from larger solids. If you had to separate a mixture of salt and rice, you could easily do it using a sieve. The grains of salt would fall through the sieve, leaving the rice behind.

Separating a solid from a liquid

If you add soil to a jar of water and stir it, the particles of soil mix with the water. You can see them floating around. If you leave the jar undisturbed, the soil will slowly sink and settle on the bottom of the jar. You can then separate the soil from most of the water by carefully pouring the water away. This is called decanting.

A tea strainer has a finer mesh than a colander. It separates the tea leaves from the tea.

You can sometimes separate solids from a liquid by straining. A colander is a kind of sieve. It is used in the kitchen to drain rice, peas and other foods that have been cooked in water.

A sieve separates smaller pieces. Tea is sometimes made in a teapot by pouring boiling water over loose tea leaves. To stop the tea leaves getting into the cup, the tea is poured through a sieve or tea strainer.

Exploring further – Solids and liquids

To find out more about separating solids and liquids, follow this path on the CD-ROM: Contents > Quick Facts > Separating solids and liquids

Filters

A **filter** is like a very fine sieve. It can separate **solid** powders from **liquids**. One way to separate a **mixture** of soil and water is to pour it through a filter paper. The filter lets the water through, but holds back the soil. Many filters are made of paper.

Filter papers

Coffee is sometimes made by pouring boiling water over freshly ground coffee beans. The ground beans are put in a funnel lined with a filter paper. The boiling water is poured into the funnel and mixes with the coffee grains. Some of the coffee is **dissolved** in the water and drips through to the pot below, while the hard remains of the beans are left in the filter paper.

Coffee filters make sure that no grains of coffee are poured into the cup.

Scientists also use filter papers to separate solids from liquids, such as crystals that form in **solutions**. In a car engine, a filter in the carburettor removes dust and other solid particles from the air. The air is then drawn into the cylinders to burn the petrol.

A tea-bag is a filter paper wrapped around a portion of tea leaves. When boiling water is poured over the bag, the water passes through the paper filter and mixes with the tea leaves inside, taking in the flavour of the tea.

Other kinds of filters

Filters can be made of cloth, charcoal or any material that allows liquid to run through it. People who make their own jam often strain it through a piece of fine cloth called muslin. Straining removes all the pips and tiny bits of fruit so that, when the jam sets, it will be a clear jelly.

Filters made of fabric are used in vacuum cleaners to separate the dust from the air it is sucked up with. Air-conditioners also use filters made of fabric to remove solid particles from the air.

In a sewage works water trickles through a filter bed to clean it.

Water filters

Water must be cleaned before it is piped to our homes from rivers or reservoirs. First the largest solids are left to settle to the bottom. The rest of the water is then passed through a filter bed. The filter bed consists of a thick layer of sand or of sand and coal on top of a thick layer of gravel. As the water trickles through the filter bed, most of the solid particles of dirt are filtered out. The water is then piped away and treated to kill any germs.

Exploring further – Water to drink

Water goes through many filtration processes before we can drink it. How do know that the water that comes from the tap is clean and safe? Follow this path on the CD-ROM to find out: Contents> Digging Deeper > Separating materials > Clean water

Separating a solution

Some **solids** mix so well with a **liquid** that they **dissolve**. If you add salt to water and stir it, the grains of salt dissolve and disappear. The salt mixes so well with the water that it becomes part of the liquid. Something that dissolves in a liquid is called a **solute**. A **solvent** is a liquid in which something dissolves. A solute and solvent mix together to form a **solution**.

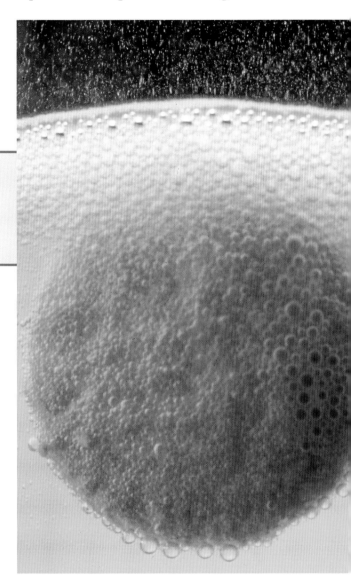

The orange tablet contains vitamin C. It is dissolved in water to make it easier to swallow.

Soluble or insoluble

Things which dissolve are said to be **soluble**. Many things are soluble in water. Sugar dissolves in hot tea (which is mainly water) to make sweet tea. Some painkillers dissolve in water to make them easier to take. Things that do not dissolve are said to be insoluble. Sand and rice are insoluble in water.

Evaporating a solution

You cannot separate a solute from a solvent by sieving it or by **filtering** it. In a solution, the solid becomes part of the liquid and so passes through a sieve or filter along with it. To separate a solute from a solution you have to **evaporate** the liquid.

If you leave a solution of salt in a saucer in a warm place, the water will slowly evaporate. As it evaporates, the solution becomes more and more concentrated. Eventually all the water evaporates, leaving behind crystals of salt. Heating a solution makes the solvent evaporate faster. Heating salty water soon produces salt crystals. Another way of making salt water evaporate faster is to pour it into a bigger dish. This increases the surface area of the solution. Blowing hot air from a hairdryer across the surface will speed up the process too.

Other solvents

Hair spray is a laquer (a kind of **varnish**), dissolved in a solvent and sold in **airtight** cans. As soon as it is sprayed onto someone's hair, the solvent evaporates, leaving behind the lacquer.

When you paint your nails with nail varnish, you have to wait a minute or two for the varnish to dry. The solvent in the varnish evaporates, leaving behind a layer of hard, shiny varnish.

Exploring further – Separating mixtures of materials

Do you know what happens if you leave a solution of salt in a warm place? To see an animation of water evaporating, follow this path on the CD-ROM: Contents > Key Ideas > Separating mixtures of materials

Separating in stages

Sometimes a **mixture** is separated in stages, using several different methods. For example, if you wanted to get drinkable water and salt from sea water, you would have to separate it in two stages. First you would have to remove any sand or other **solid** particles, and then you would have to separate the salt from the water in which it was **dissolved**.

Removing the sand

The first stage would be to separate out any sand or other solid particles present by pouring the mixture through a **filter** into a bowl or jug. The salt **solution** passes through the filter paper and collects in the bowl, while the sand is left behind. If you wanted to keep the sand, you could leave the filter paper to dry and then shake the sand off.

A mixture of water, salt and . sand is poured through a filter. The filter separates the sand from the solution of salt and water.

Removing the water

You separate the water from the salt by **evaporating** the water from the solution. If you want to keep the water, you need to find some way of changing the water **vapour** back into a **liquid**. Scientists use a condenser, which is a tube surrounded by cold water, to do this. The change from vapour to liquid is called **condensation**. Look at the picture on page 43 to see how a condenser works.

Distilling

In industry, many solutions and mixtures are separated using evaporation and condensation. This process is called **distillation**. Water from wells, rivers and reservoirs is distilled to produce pure water. Distilled water is used in car batteries and steam irons. In an **oil** refinery, crude oil is distilled to separate it into several different substances. These substances are used to produce petrol, medicines, plastics, paints and many other products.

The solution is heated in a flask until the water starts to evaporate and change into water vapour. The water vapour tries to escape but cannot, so it is forced into the condenser. The condenser is cold because it is surrounded by cold water. Water from a tap goes in through a tube at one end and out of another tube at the other end. Because it is constantly flowing it stays cold. When the hot gas reaches the cold condenser, it condenses back into a liquid and drips into the beaker below. When all the water has evaporated, the salt is left at the bottom of the flask.

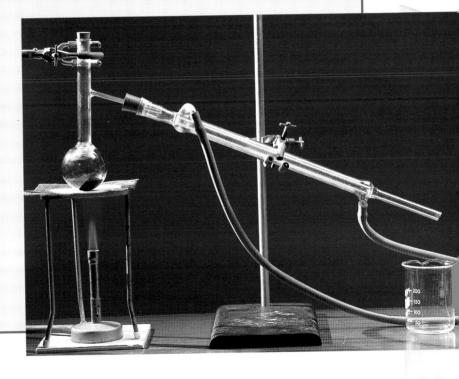

Exploring further – Electrolysis

Some materials are so tightly bound together that they can only be torn apart using electricity. This is called electrolysis. To learn how this happens, follow this path: Contents > Digging Deeper > Separating materials < Electrolysis

What do scientists do?

Scientists want to know more about the world and how to look after it. They ask questions about all the things in our world that affect how we live, how comfortable we are and how we keep healthy. For hundreds of years, scientists have studied plants, animals and materials and tried to find out why certain things happen.

We all need to understand about science and how a scientist works. To become a good scientist you will need to be curious about the things you use, the things you see and the things that happen around you.

Part of being a scientist is asking questions. Some of these questions can be answered by reading books and using CD-ROMs and the Internet.

Sometimes you will want to find out the answer by doing a scientific investigation. You will need to collect information and use this to try to give

an answer to your question. Sometimes our questions are not answered and we need to try again with a different investigation.

Once you have collected your information, you need to record it. Then you will need to think about what your results mean and what you can learn from them.

Doing all these things can help you to learn more about the world. When you can understand how important it is to carry out the scientific process correctly, then you will be well on your way to becoming a good scientist.

Exploring further

Learn more about how to be a scientist from the CD-ROM. The Scientific Enquiry section will show you how to plan your investigations and how to collect and think about your results. The Heinemann Explore website can give you many further areas to explore: **www.heinemannexplore.co.uk**

Weblinks

You can find out more about this area of science by looking at the Weblinks on the CD-ROM. Here is a selection of sites available:

www.exploratorium.edu/science_explorer
How would a physicist put ketchup on his chips? What makes a lava lamp work? How does a shadow tell time? These questions are answered in simple scientific experiments that you can try at home.

www.ncsu.edu/sciencejunction/station/experiments/EGG/egg.html
A set of three fun home experiments using eggs. What happens to eggs in acid? Can substances pass through the shell? How do forces affect the motion of objects?

www.nyu.edu/pages/mathmol/textbook/elem_home1.html
A selection of pages dealing with a number of topics in chemistry including water, matter and energy, and atoms and molecules.

The CD-ROM contains a large selection of useful weblinks. Just click on the weblinks button at the edge of the screen.

Further reading

Solids, Liquids and Gases, Robert Snedden, Heinemann Library, Oxford: 2001
Materials and Their Properties, Karen Bryant-Mole, Heinemann Library, Oxford: 2001
Changing Materials, Robert Snedden, Heinemann Library, Oxford: 2001
What is the World Made Of? All about Solids, Liquids and Gases, Kathleen Weidner Zoehfeld, Harper Collins, London: 1998

Glossary

absorb to take in or soak up

airtight not allowing air to pass through

atmosphere air – the mixture of gases that surrounds the Earth

atom tiny particle from which all materials are made; the smallest part of an element that can exist

biodegradable able to be rotted down into natural elements by bacteria

boil 1. to make a liquid so hot that it begins to change rapidly into a gas
2. to cook by boiling

boiling point temperature at which a material changes from a liquid to a gas and from a gas to a liquid

carbon dioxide gas that is found in the air; it is produced when fuels burn and when plants and animals breathe out

chemical change a change that cannot be reversed or undone; a change that alters the chemicals in a substance

chemical reaction a reaction that takes place between two or more substances in which energy is given out or taken in and new substances are produced

chemicals substances that can join together and mix with other substances

condensation when a gas cools and changes into a liquid

condense to change from a gas or vapour into a liquid

conduct/conductor substance that allows heat or electricity to pass through it

coniferous trees that produce cones with seeds instead of flowers

deciduous trees that shed their leaves annually

dilute make a solution weaker by adding more solvent

dissolve to mix a solid or a gas with a liquid so thoroughly that it becomes liquid too

distillation way of separating a pure liquid from a mixture

evaporate to change from a liquid into a gas or vapour

evaporation occurs when a liquid warms up and changes into a gas

fabric a cloth that is made by weaving, knitting or felting

fibre thread of material that can be spun into a longer, stronger thread

filter 1. to separate a solid from a liquid by pouring the liquid through a filter
2. device for separating solids from a liquid

freeze change from a liquid to a solid

freezing point temperature at which a liquid freezes and becomes solid

fuel substance that people burn to make heat or light, or to make engines work. Wood is a fuel. So are gas and petrol.

gas substance in a state where it spreads out into all the space it can

global warming an increase in the temperature of the Earth's atmosphere

hardwood wood, such as oak, walnut or mahogany, that comes from broad-leafed, deciduous trees

hygienic keeping things clean for reasons of health

insulator material that does not allow heat or electricity to pass through it

irreversible when something, such as change to a material, cannot be undone

liquid substance in a runny state which can be poured from one container to another

magnet anything that attracts iron or steel to it

matter anything that takes up space and has weight. Matter can be solid, liquid or gas

melt to change from a solid into a liquid due to heat

melting point temperature at which a solid turns into a liquid

metal a type of mineral that is a good conductor of heat and electricity

mixture when two or more substances are mixed together but can be separated

molecule smallest part of a substance that can exist and still be that substance

molten turned into liquid by heat

natural found in or produced by nature

natural gas gas found underground

nylon strong, synthetic material with flexible threads used to make yarn, fabric, fishing rods, etc.

oil thick, black liquid found underground or under the sea. We get lots of useful chemicals from oil. Some are used to make plastics. Petrol for cars also comes from oil.

ore metal combined with another substance, as it is found in rocks

oxygen gas that makes up a fifth of the air; animals need to breathe oxygen to survive

physical change change that can be undone or reversed; a change that does not alter the chemicals in a substance

plastic 1. substance made in a factory, that may be shaped when soft and then hardened
2. something that stays in its new shape after it is pulled or stretched – it does not go back to how it was before

pollutant a substance that poisons the air, water or land

properties qualities or characteristics of a substance or material

rayon synthetic fabric used in clothing. It dries quickly but melts easily.

reversible when something, such as a change to material, can be undone

rust when iron or steel combines with the oxygen in water or damp air to form an orange powder

sap fluid inside plants

saturated full up and unable to take in any more of a substance

silicon a non-metallic element - the most plentiful solid element on Earth

softwood wood that comes from coniferous trees, such as pine and spruce

solid an object having a definite shape

solidify change from a liquid into a solid

soluble able to be dissolved

solute substance that dissolves in a liquid to form a solution

solution liquid obtained when a substance dissolves in a solvent

solvent liquid in which a substance dissolves

state form that something takes - materials can be solid, liquid or gas

suspended when particles float in a liquid or gas

synthetic material material that is not found naturally but is made from another substance, usually oil. Plastic is the most common synthetic material.

temperature measure of how hot or cold something is

thermal to do with heat

thermometer instrument that measures temperature

vapour gas

varnish liquid coating that dries and leaves a glossy, transparent look when you put it on a surface

Index

Titles in the *Explore Science* series include:

Hardback   0 431 17440 7

Hardback   0 431 17441 5

Hardback   0 431 17442 3

Find out about the other titles in this series on our website www.heinemann.co.uk/library